LISA PARRY

Lisa Parry is a playwright based in Cardiff. Her play *The Merthyr Stigmatist* was shortlisted for Theatre Uncut's inaugural Political Playwriting Award in 2019, a prize supported by the Sherman, Traverse and Young Vic. She was a writer-in-residence at Theatr Clwyd in 2020.

Lisa's work has been staged by leading new-writing companies in the UK and USA, including Dirty Protest, The Miniaturists and PopUp Theatrics. Her work has been produced at the Barbican, The Other Room, Wales Millennium Centre, Chapter Arts, Theatre503, the Arcola, TACT Studio (Broadway, NYC), the Arches, Bridewell Theatre and Martin E. Segal Theatre Center (NYC).

In 2016, Lisa co-founded Illumine Theatre Company with director Zoë Waterman. The company's first production – of Lisa's play *2023* – opened to rave reviews in October 2018. *Wales Arts Review* described it as 'wonderfully written', *Art Scene in Wales* called it 'a truly thought-provoking piece', and *Get the Chance* described it as '[a] stunning new play… I propose that it is in the running for best Welsh play of 2018.'

Lisa has spoken extensively on various panels regarding feminism and theatre and also science and theatre, notably giving a talk for TEDx in Cardiff. She co-produced work by female playwrights across the UK for Agent 160 Theatre Company in 2012 and 2014 – a company she co-founded – in response to the statistic that just seventeen per cent of produced plays were then written by women. Lisa previously worked as a news journalist on regional and national titles and was an associate editor (theatre) on *Bare Fiction Magazine*.

Lisa is currently under commission from Theatr Clwyd and researching a new play, supported by the Peggy Ramsay Foundation.

Lisa Parry

THE MERTHYR STIGMATIST

NICK HERN BOOKS

London

www.nickhernbooks.co.uk

A Nick Hern Book

The Merthyr Stigmatist first published in Great Britain in 2021 as a paperback original by Nick Hern Books Limited, The Glasshouse, 49a Goldhawk Road, London W12 8QP, in association with Sherman Theatre and Theatre Uncut

The Merthyr Stigmatist copyright © 2021 Lisa Parry

Lisa Parry has asserted her moral right to be identified as the author of this work

Cover image: Burning Red

Designed and typeset by Nick Hern Books, London
Printed in the UK by Mimeo Ltd, Huntingdon, Cambridgeshire PE29 6XX

A CIP catalogue record for this book is available from the British Library

ISBN 978 1 83904 005 4

Woodland
CARBON
www.woodlandcarbon.co.uk
NICK HERN BOOKS
Printed on Carbon Captured paper

Introduction

Emma Callander, director of The Merthyr Stigmatist
and Co-Artistic Director of Theatre Uncut

This play gave me shivers when I first read it. The voice of this sixteen-year-old girl from Merthyr Tydfil was fighting to get off the page. It felt fiercely political. Carys's connection to her home town is visceral, its blood pumps through her veins. The prejudice directed towards Merthyr physically hurts. She reflects teenage girls from post-industrial towns across the world.

Once an industrial world leader in coal, steel and iron production, Merthyr Tydfil has had to adapt to an increasingly globalised manufacturing landscape and seen so many of its collieries and factories close and job opportunities dwindle. The spirit of rebellion has always been strong in Merthyr from the nineteenth-century Merthyr Rising, right through to the inspiring attitudes of the students of Merthyr College today. We want to say a particular thank you to the students who helped us throughout the development of this play and their powerhouse course leader Kayleigh Adlam.

Hannah Price and I from Theatre Uncut were honoured that Lisa chose to submit this wild play to the inaugural Theatre Uncut Political Playwriting Award, and we are delighted to present it with Sherman Theatre in this, our tenth anniversary year. Theatre Uncut was created for everyone everywhere to engage with political new writing, so we are releasing an extended monologue to accompany this premiere performance to give young Welsh actresses a resource to support their own creative journeys. You can find this monologue at the back of this publication.

Thank you for entrusting me with this play, Lisa. And thank you to the cast, creative team, crew and Sherman staff for showing such dedication and care in bringing it to the stage. It feels good to be back in the theatre.

May 2021

The Merthyr Stigmatist received its world premiere as a fully staged co-production between Sherman Theatre and Theatre Uncut which was released on demand and online on 27 May 2021.

Cafodd *The Merthyr Stigmatist* ei lwyfannu'n llawn am y tro cyntaf mewn cyd-gynhyrchiad rhwng Theatr y Sherman a Theatre Uncut, ac fe'i rhyddhawyd ar alw ac ar-lein ar Fai 27 2021.

SIÂN	Bethan Mary-James
CARYS	Bethan McLean
Director / Cyfarwyddwr	Emma Callander
Designer / Cynllunydd	Elin Steele
Composer / Cyfansoddwr	Eädyth Crawford
Sound Designer /	
Cynllunydd Sain	Ian Barnard
Lighting Designer /	
Cynllunydd Goleuo	Andy Pike
Assistant Director /	
Cyfarwyddwr Cynorthwyol	Carli De'La Hughes
Fight Director /	
Cyfarwyddwr Ymladd	Kev McCurdy
Assistant Stage Manager /	
Rheolwr Llwyfan Cynorthwyol	Alys Robinson
Deputy Stage Manager /	
Dirprwy Rheolwr Llwyfan	Ailsa Bonner

Acknowledgements

Thanks to Theatre Uncut for setting up this award, the Sherman, Traverse and Young Vic for supporting it, and to all the people who read this play as a really early draft and who saw enough in it to keep putting it through – I could not be more humbled or grateful; to all the wonderful actors who helped with its development at the Sherman – Holly Carpenter, Rebecca Harries, Charlotte O'Leary, Sian Reese-Williams – and to the staff and students of The College, Merthyr Tydfil/Y Coleg Merthyr Tudful for being so open, inspiring and engaged; to Theatr Clwyd for giving me space and time to finish a crucial draft just before the craziness of lockdown hit; to everyone at the Sherman, especially Julia Barry, Timothy Howe, Ceriann Williams and Joe Murphy, for his belief and dramaturgy; to Emma Callander for her knack in pushing me forward whilst determinedly protecting the play's initial spark; to Cardiff Arms Park Male Choir and Kris Crowley and Kinetic Theatre Arts for lending us your incredible voices; to my brilliant agent Micheline Steinberg and everyone at Micheline Steinberg Associates, and to Matt Applewhite and everyone at Nick Hern Books for trusting in the play and in me. Finally, a huge thanks to the playwrights of Wales, once described by the talented and much-missed Othniel Smith as 'an undervalued and marginalised but resilient species', for their constant encouragement and support. *Diolch o galon.*

L.P.

For Nick

Characters

CARYS, *sixteen*
SIÂN, *her teacher*

Notes on Dialogue

[ ] denotes intended but unspoken speech.

… denotes a pause for thought or speech trailing off.

/ denotes overlapping dialogue and the point of interruption.

– denotes a non-verbal response from a character to the preceding line.

This text went to press before the end of rehearsals and so may differ slightly from the play as performed.

Friday, 3.05 p.m. A classroom in a Catholic secondary school, Merthyr Tydfil, Wales. We're a couple of weeks into the summer term. A high, narrow window is open. CARYS *has clean bandages wrapped around both hands. She is wearing a smart watch, concealed from the audience and* SIÂN.

CARYS. Do you have pills in your bag, Miss?

SIÂN. Do I look like a dealer?

CARYS. I mean paracetamol. Bloody hell. Do you though?

SIÂN. I'm not giving you drugs, Carys.

CARYS. But my hands are killin'!

SIÂN. Tough.

> *Beat.*

CARYS. Mr Brooks is the one meant to be doing detentions today, it says so on the rota.

SIÂN. But you have me instead. Lucky you.

> *Beat.*

CARYS. Can I go home?

SIÂN. Answer those questions.

CARYS. But I need to get ready! I'm meeting Candice. We're going to see if we can get into Koolers – her cousin's just got a job on the door.

SIÂN. Write, Carys.

> CARYS *does for a little while, then stops.*

CARYS. Don't you want to go out too, Miss? Pop out for a cheeky 'Spoons like.

SIÂN. No. Some of us are busy.

CARYS. But it'd do you good – getting out of the house for a bit. It's not healthy, living in your mam's stuff like that.

SIÂN. What?

CARYS. What? Charity Jean said you haven't dropped a single bag off at Oxfam yet. I think she has her eye on a couple of your mam's cardies to be honest.

SIÂN. Be quiet, Carys.

CARYS. We're looking out for you, Miss, that's all.

SIÂN. I'm a grown woman, I can look out for myself.

Beat.

CARYS. These questions are boring.

SIÂN. I wrote that exam paper, thank you very much.

CARYS. That doesn't make them not boring. How long am I here for?

SIÂN. Let me see what you've put.

CARYS *passes the papers to* SIÂN.

Is this a joke?

CARYS. No.

SIÂN. Question One: Describe a vibration. You've put 'There are good vibrations and bad vibrations. Good vibrations were discovered in the 1960s.'

CARYS. That's good music knowledge that is. Retro.

SIÂN. Question Two: Describe the formation and chemical structure of a diamond. You've put 'Shirley Bassey says diamonds are forever so the structure must be well good.'

SIÂN *drops the papers on* CARYS*'s table.*

I don't have time for this.

CARYS. Then let me go home. I don't want to be stuck here answering science questions, mun.

SIÂN. Course you don't. They get you to think.

CARYS. Yeah, cos science is the only subject that can do that.

SIÂN. I'm a science teacher, what else am I going to set you?

CARYS. I dunno, Religious Studies maybe?

SIÂN. Do the work I've set.

CARYS. The school putting me in detention like this is so illegal.

SIÂN. Illegal, really?

CARYS. It's twenty-four hours' notice and a letter home.

SIÂN. That's school policy. Legally, we don't have to give notice at all.

CARYS. This is mental! What have I done that's so bad?

Beat.

This place is a joke. The detention I got last week? That wasn't fair either.

SIÂN. I gave you that detention because you were playing truant.

CARYS. I never! I was in Prince Charles!

SIÂN. I know – wasting their time. Don't you think that hospital's busy enough right now without you walking in like the second coming?

CARYS. My wounds got infected they did. Think long term, Miss – I can't even sit the exams if my hands and feet drop off, can I? And they would have too if I'd got sepsis.

SIÂN. You didn't have sepsis.

CARYS. No, but I was right to get it checked. It was the doctor off the telly I saw, the one they interview with the valleys in the background. You know the one – he has this look in his eye, like he wants to remind everyone we're here, fight the good fight. It's dead sexy, Miss.

Beat.

Why am I here?

Beat.

Do you know why I'm here?

Beat.

You can't keep me here. I have the right not to be separated from my mam and nan. Article 9, UN convention on the rights of the child.

SIÂN. What are you on about?

CARYS. You should read it, Miss. Library in town's got one. Bryn Books on the issue desk will sort you out.

SIÂN *gets a text on her phone.*

SIÂN. We'll be staying a while longer.

CARYS. I can't! It's Friday!

SIÂN. Not everything in the world revolves around you, Carys. You won't get into Koolers. Whoever's on the door will take one look at you and see you're just a child.

CARYS. It's not that, Miss.

SIÂN. What then?

CARYS. It hasn't happened yet. It happens every Friday.

SIÂN. You'll be fine.

CARYS. It's not just my hands that bleed any more, it's my feet now too.

SIÂN. I'm not listening to this.

CARYS. Miss!

SIÂN. What do you want me to say? Seriously, Carys, what? Nothing is going to happen because nothing ever happens. The wounds of Christ do not magically appear on your body each Friday like some kind of freakish Harry Potter scar; the blood of Jesus does not gush out of your hands and feet.

CARYS *marches to the laptop.*

What are you doing?

CARYS. Showing you I'm not lying.

SIÂN. Leave my laptop alone!

　　CARYS *types again.*

CARYS. I am showing you, proving to you that…

SIÂN. Proving what?

CARYS. There. Proof I'm telling the truth.

　　A video plays. SIÂN *watches as much of it as she can stomach.*

Does that look like I do it to myself?

　　SIÂN *watches* CARYS *watching the video.*

Miss! Did you see? It's got five thousand likes already! Five thousand and three, five thousand and five!

SIÂN. Delete it.

CARYS. Catholics in the Valleys have shared it, did you see? Dai Twice is so lush. Mr Davies from church? David Davies so Dai Twice? Jesus, Miss. It might have six thousand likes now. Let's check.

SIÂN. No!

CARYS. Why?

SIÂN. I don't want you near it.

CARYS. The likes won't go to my head. Though right now I reckon I'm the most famous person from Dowlais since Laura Ashley. Do you know how many people live in Merthyr, Miss? I mean – all of Merthyr?

SIÂN. No.

CARYS. Serious? It's about sixty thousand. Can you imagine if it got that many likes, Miss? I'd be such a celeb, mun. I'd be Jesus on Wi-Fi.

SIÂN. Imagine what could happen if someone at *The Express* sees it!

CARYS. That'd be epic!

SIÂN. No, it wouldn't! Switch it off now, Carys.

CARYS. Alright.

Unseen by SIÂN, CARYS *quickly types a comment and posts it. Unseen by* CARYS, SIÂN *locks the door.*

You okay, Miss? You look a bit peaky.

SIÂN. How long's that been online?

CARYS. A couple of hours.

SIÂN. Who helped you do that?

CARYS. No one. I know it looks dead professional like, but I didn't even use a filter.

SIÂN. Even for you, Carys, this is another level.

CARYS. I know. It's amazing. If you ignore the blood in it, Miss, I look quite fit.

SIÂN. Is this what you want to be known for? Half the school's calling you Carys Christ already.

CARYS. CC for short, like Coco Chanel.

SIÂN. You are so irresponsible.

CARYS. Irresponsible?

SIÂN. Kids will see that!

CARYS. I'm a kid.

SIÂN. Younger, impressionable kids who genuinely need help.

Beat.

CARYS. You don't believe me, do you? Even after that, you still… What do I have to do? Do I have to literally bleed in front of you? Nothing I do will ever be good enough for you, will it? I'm done, mun.

SIÂN. Carys!

CARYS *tries to open the door.*

CARYS.The door's locked. Why's the door locked?

SIÂN. Carys…

CARYS. Did you do that?

SIÂN. Sit down.

CARYS. Sit down? It's not normal to lock a classroom door!

CARYS *bangs on the door.*

Help! Help me!

SIÂN. Stop being such a drama queen. School's finished now, no one can hear.

CARYS. This is a Catholic school! Is there a secret room under the floorboards? Are priests going to come in / and…

SIÂN. Don't be ridiculous!

CARYS. I'm not! Stuff like that's happened, mun!

SIÂN. This is your school in Merthyr and you are safe.

CARYS. I want to know who locked the door! Was it Big Willy? That man is such / a…

SIÂN. His name is Mr Williams. He's the headteacher, you should show some respect.

CARYS. He's a complete and utter knobhead! And you agreed to it? Have you gone psycho, Miss?

SIÂN. I've not gone psycho.

CARYS. That's what someone who's gone psycho would say though.

SIÂN *gets another text.*

Is that him? What's he saying then? Has he got some master plan for me?

SIÂN. I… I don't know.

CARYS. For someone who's agreed to lock a kid in a room, you don't know a lot, do you? You've not thought this through. I could say you'd done anything in here and you'd be well fucked. Tell him to let me go. Nothing bad's going to happen cos Jesus sends me his wounds each week, is it? I'm under God's protection.

SIÂN. No, I'm your form teacher and you're under mine.

CARYS. No offence, Miss, but I think God might be better at this safeguarding stuff than you.

SIÂN. Why? You think he's going to zap away stalkers with lightning bolts, do you?

CARYS. Why not? *He* cares, Miss. He'll keep me safe because I'm doing what he wants.

SIÂN. Which is what?

CARYS. Showing we can be chosen, showing we matter!

SIÂN. Matter to who?

CARYS. To him cos he's sent this. Is it the grief, Miss? Stopping you thinking clearly, is it?

SIÂN. I caught three Year 7 girls gouging flesh out of their hands and feet with scissors this afternoon so they could look like you.

Beat.

CARYS. What?

SIÂN. Is that helping? Is that showing everyone we matter?

CARYS. Who were they?

SIÂN. I can't say.

CARYS. Don't be daft. I'll find out anyway, you know I will.

SIÂN. They're eleven years old and they were bleeding. You need help now. This has to stop! Why are you doing this? I mean, really? Is it to please your nan?

CARYS. No! She'd never ask me / to…

SIÂN. Is it money?

CARYS. How could this have anything to do with / money?

SIÂN. Kids in Business Studies are working out how much profit they'll make from 'Canonise Carys' T-shirts.

CARYS. That has nothing to do with me!

SIÂN. Do you like being talked about?

Beat.

CARYS. Look at me! I'm walking around with wounds!

SIÂN. Which you're doing to yourself.

CARYS. Does it matter?

SIÂN. What?

CARYS. Does it really matter if I'm doing it to myself or not?

SIÂN. Of course it matters!

CARYS. Why does it? If it gets people to listen – it's still a miracle, isn't it?

SIÂN. Please understand, you can stop; I can help you stop! This is your mental health we're talking about – it's serious!

CARYS. My mental health is fine! I'm not like Gruff. His arms are like train tracks now. He adds lines in the field at dinner while you're all sat in the staffroom, flirting and eating your edamame-bean salads and congratulating yourselves on having jobs.

SIÂN. The school is dealing with Gruff.

CARYS. This is not about me.

SIÂN. Carys, there's no shame in admitting you're self-harming. I know how to help! Let me help you.

Pause.

CARYS. You can't do it, can you?

SIÂN. Can't do what?

CARYS. Can't think for one second that it's real, that I might know more about something than you do, even though it's actually happening to me. What will it take to get you to listen properly to what I'm saying?

SIÂN. What will it take to get me to believe this is a real stigmata? Are you serious?

CARYS. Yeah.

SIÂN. Proof.

CARYS. I showed you a video!

SIÂN. And I saw a performance, not divine intervention! Seriously, Carys, that's not proof! Let's follow your logic. Let's say those marks are from God, whether you put them there or not.

CARYS. I never said I put them there, Miss.

SIÂN. If you're right, if this whole thing is a gift from God – get him to give me a sign and I'll listen to you. In fact – get him to do it now.

CARYS. That's not fair.

SIÂN. Why?

CARYS. You're not meant to test God. It says so in the Bible.

SIÂN. Oh please. That's a get-out clause and you know it. God's omniscient, isn't he – all-seeing and knowing? So he can hear me asking. And you think he's great at safeguarding you so I'm sure he'll come through. Ask him, go on. I'm waiting.

Silence. Then singing is heard from outside – 'Cwm Rhondda'.

CARYS. He so just dropped the mic on you, Miss.

SIÂN. What is that?

CARYS. Isn't it obvious?

CARYS *looks out of the window.*

SIÂN. You think God's sent singing angels or something for you now, do you?

CARYS. No, I think it's a proper male voice choir.

SIÂN. Don't be [stupid].

CARYS. It's the Abercanaid one. Dai Post runs it. He told Nan it might stop some of the blokes getting depressed.

SIÂN. Why would they come here?

CARYS. Because God knew what you were going to say. He moved them to come and sing.

SIÂN. Carys, be serious!

CARYS. I am! Fuck. I actually am, Miss!

SIÂN. Someone's told them you're here. Carys?

CARYS. Maybe it was Candice.

SIÂN. Candice?

CARYS. Yeah.

SIÂN. How?

CARYS. She was nagging me to go to the retail park with her after school so she could buy a new top in case she sees Owen Peters later. She was tampin' when you came and got me. Maybe she rang the choir to flush me out.

SIÂN. Maybe Candice rang Abercanaid Male Voice Choir so she could pull Owen Peters?

CARYS. I wouldn't put it past her. Mad for him she is.

SIÂN. Carys – you don't treat me like an idiot, understand?

CARYS. Or maybe…

SIÂN. What?

CARYS. I left a comment on Dai Twice's page when we looked at it. Maybe it was that.

SIÂN. Saying?

CARYS. That you were keeping me in school illegally.

SIÂN. You did what?

CARYS. Listen to them, Miss! They want me to know I'm not alone. They believe me so much, they're singing to prove it.

SIÂN *shuts the window.*

SIÂN. Why do you always have to make everything so difficult?

CARYS. I don't!

SIÂN. They won't be there long. Mr Harris will be on his way to move them.

CARYS. Why will he? They're not doing any harm!

SIÂN. They shouldn't be on school property. It's trespass. If they won't go, he'll have to call the police.

CARYS. Call the police on a choir? You serious?

SIÂN. Do I look like I'm joking?

CARYS. Mr Harris might ask them to go but he won't call the police, mun.

SIÂN. He will if he has to. It's his job, Carys.

CARYS. How long have you been working here, Miss?

SIÂN. Three months, why?

CARYS. And how many times have drain covers been stolen from the yard since you started?

SIÂN. Two.

CARYS. And was there any sign of forced entry on either occasion?

SIÂN. What are you saying?

CARYS. Mr Harris's brother's Universal Credit got stopped after he missed his appointment taking his kid to Prince Charles. Mr Harris won't want the police here, will he, mun? No way will he call them.

SIÂN. That's a serious accusation.

CARYS. Getting evicted when you've a kid's serious too. There was no harm done, not really. We all just look where we're going on the yard more now. He's the best caretaker ever, Mr Harris. He cares.

SIÂN. This place, sometimes I literally can't [get my head around it].

CARYS. Yeah, well that's cos you're different now, aren't you? With your fake Cardiff accent. We look after each other here. Maybe you'd remember, if you let people help.

SIÂN. Them? Those people out there, they don't care about you! Not really, not long term. Think about your future, would you? Your exams start in less than a month!

CARYS. I know and I'm trying. But I've been a bit distracted.

SIÂN. Well, stop! This is the most important year of your life so far and your schoolwork should / be your top priority.

CARYS (*mimics*).... 'and your schoolwork should be your top priority'. Do you think that's what Our Lady should have done, Miss – said to Gabriel she was fine to get knocked up with Jesus but only after her GCSEs?

SIÂN. Do you want to throw your life away over this? Is that really what you want? If you work hard, in two years you could go to university.

CARYS. Has it ever occurred to you, Miss, that I might not want to go?

SIÂN. You keep saying that, but you will.

CARYS. No, I won't! Why would I when I like it here? I don't want to live somewhere that could be anywhere, with the same shops and cafés, selling the same coffee, drunk by people all wearing the same type of clothes.

SIÂN. Moving away would be good for you.

CARYS. Why?

SIÂN. It'd be a fresh start.

CARYS. Yeah, one where I could show everyone just how clever I am by taking on loads of debt. I'm not going to abandon my home like you did.

SIÂN. Carys, when I went to uni, I moved forty minutes down the A470.

CARYS. Get real, Miss. Cardiff's a different world. You couldn't get away fast enough when your dad died.

SIÂN. Who told you that?

CARYS. Your mam.

Beat.

She was close to my nan. My nan's Luce Richards. She runs the Catholic Women's League at church. She did the altar flowers for your mam's funeral. Added loads of lilies to them. She said your dad used to buy your mam lilies on her birthday so she thought it'd be a nice touch, a way of remembering him too like. They were selling them off cheap at M&S anyway after St Dwynwen's Day. Not much take-up.

SIÂN. I didn't abandon my home.

CARYS. You only came back when she was dying; you didn't have much choice.

SIÂN. I'm here now.

CARYS. Only because she left you the house. You're not really here properly, are you? You keep well back from everyone. Worried your accent might come back, are you? Scared what that'd make people think? I reckon you're only here cos you don't know what to do if you leave. So don't walk around thinking we should be grateful, Miss. Don't expect a fucking medal cos you're stuck.

Beat.

SIÂN *uses the laptop.*

What are you doing?

SIÂN. Finding someone to get through to you.

CARYS. You serious?

SIÂN. You won't listen to me.

Beat.

This is logged in as Mr Williams.

CARYS. Best not check his history, Miss. It's not great.

SIÂN. Did you do this? Carys?

CARYS. I couldn't get in as me – my login's suspended.

SIÂN. But how did you know his password?

CARYS. We all know it.

SIÂN. How? We change them each week.

CARYS. Yeah but Big Willy just works down a list of Welsh saints he's got pinned up in his office.

Why won't you let me go home? Can I go if I promise not to kill myself? Please? How about if I pinky promise?

I don't mean to state the obvious, Miss, but you're going to struggle to find anyone. It's Friday. The Four Horsemen of the Apocalypse could be riding into town down Brecon Road about now and that lot would still be fucking off early for a weekend in the Gower.

SIÂN *dials.*

Who's first up then?

SIÂN. Your social worker.

CARYS. Danielle? Good luck with that. It's the third Friday of the month – she'll be getting her gels done.

SIÂN (*on the phone*). Hello, is Danielle Evans available please? Thank you. (*To* CARYS.) They've gone to find her. (*On the phone*.) Oh, is she? Is there anyone else there I could…

CARYS (*whispers loudly*). They'll be glamping in the Gower.

SIÂN (*on the phone*). It's okay, I'll call again later.

She hangs up, searches for a number.

CARYS. Can I at least have some paracetamol? I'm not allergic!

SIÂN. No! It's school policy – I'm not allowed to give you pills.

CARYS. Is it school policy to lock a pupil in a room? I won't tell. I should take them now so they'll kick in before it starts. It's less painful that way. Please, Miss.

SIÂN. I'm a teacher, Carys, not a chemist.

CARYS *goes to the window.*

What are you doing?

CARYS. It's stuffy in here. I need some air.

CARYS *opens the window. The number of voices is increasing – male and female, young and old, singing in Welsh and English.*

SIÂN *closes the window.*

CARYS. I was enjoying that!

SIÂN. Shouldn't you be enjoying stuff like Drake?

CARYS. Please don't try and relate to me, you'll embarrass yourself.

SIÂN *dials.*

Who's next then?

SIAN. The crisis team.

CARYS. Isn't that a bit extreme?

SIÂN. After what you've done?

CARYS. Don't you read the paper? They can't keep up with the number of cases. I'd be taking a place someone else needs.

SIÂN. You need to be seen!

CARYS. But I already saw one of them when this started. She stopped the sessions because I'm fine.

SIÂN. No she didn't!

CARYS. You know nothing about it. You weren't even here then.

SIÂN. I know she could only give you six sessions because of funding and when they finished, she told your mam to keep sterilising the kitchen knives.

CARYS. Just because she does it doesn't mean I use them. And it was the school counsellor who said that, Miss. Every time she spoke to me, she'd give me the look.

SIÂN. What look?

CARYS. The look, the you're-from-Merthyr look. The I-need-to-pretend-I'm-not-judging-you look. And she kept on and on asking me what the problem was, trying to find some repressed trauma. And finally, guess what we found?

SIÂN. What?

CARYS. I don't have any. You don't need to call them.

SIÂN *hangs up and scratches her hands.*

Why don't you try my GP? If you get through, they can do something useful like prescribe me antibiotics.

SIÂN. Why won't you take this seriously?

CARYS. I do, mun! I'm going to start bleeding soon and I'm genuinely worried I can't see a first-aid kit in here. If we're still here when it happens, I'll need bandages and towels.

SIÂN. I'm not engaging with you on this, Carys.

CARYS. That won't stop it happening! It's not just a bit of blood, is it? It's like my nan says – these wounds literally killed someone. Your mam believed I wasn't doing it to myself. She told me.

SIÂN. My mam kept mouldy holy water in the back of the fridge for years.

CARYS. But you're Catholic. You teach in a Catholic school! If you don't believe in miracles, why do you go to mass? Seriously – why? You went to university. You think that means you're clever. So explain to me why you won't believe.

SIÂN. Alright. Being Catholic doesn't blot out common sense, or a belief in science. And it doesn't stop you recognising the difference between religious fervour and fact. Those marks on you aren't sent from God! They can't be!

CARYS. Everyone would have said that to Francis of Assisi at first. And Catherine of Siena. And Padre Pio. Look at them now – saints. And it's not like I'm the only one alive with it now is it? There's a baby with it in the Philippines – thousands flocked to the hospital to see him, mun.

SIÂN. What?

CARYS. I think you'd believe me if I was from somewhere like the Mumbles or Monmouth.

SIÂN. No I wouldn't!

CARYS. You'd listen to me properly then. How you're thinking about this makes no sense. Jesus grew up in Nazareth. Mary appeared in Lourdes. They were both shitholes.

SIÂN. So what are you saying? God's picked Merthyr for this because it's a shithole?

CARYS. No I'm not! Merthyr's lush! I'm just saying – why shouldn't God send a miracle to Merthyr? To offer hope? He must care about it. I mean, the town's literally named after a martyr.

SIÂN. You think God would offer hope through you? A kid who quotes Shirley Bassey on a mock science paper?

CARYS. It's not my fault he picked me and not you, Miss.

SIÂN. That's not what I'm saying!

CARYS. So what are you saying?

SIÂN. That if you want to give people here hope, you should show them you can do something with your life!

CARYS. By leaving? Well, that's a great example to set. Everyone vaguely clever will bugger off and leave the old and struggling behind.

SIÂN. Go and come back and help then. Teach.

CARYS. Like you? That's why you won't believe me isn't it? Cos you're pissed at me. You want to be held up as our saviour. The Merthyr girl who did good and came home. But they're starting to think I'm the hero, aren't they? So what was the point in leaving an old woman alone for years if God chose me?

SIÂN *scratches her hands.*

SIÂN. Enough.

CARYS. I was so excited when you started here, Miss. I'd heard so much about you. My nan said you were class at my age, really wild. And the week before you came back, your mam came to see us with some Welsh cakes in that tin of hers – the one with pictures of stamps round the side and a bird on the lid? And we all sat in the garden and she told me you wouldn't be like the rest of the teachers cos you were from here; she said you'd understand who we were and who we could be – no judgement. But I saw you smile when that cockney Mr Hopkins took the piss out of my accent. On your first day.

Beat.

You can't find anyone to come.

SIÂN. No. No, I can't.

CARYS. Get Big Willy to let me go then.

Beat.

SIÂN. The school's plan seems to be that you should talk to a priest.

CARYS. Father Casey?

SIÂN. Yes.

CARYS. Okay. Well, at least he'll believe me if he's seen the video.

SIÂN. Or maybe he'll pretend to. He could do with mass numbers going up now he needs to fix the roof.

CARYS. That's harsh! You don't want me to see him. Why?

SIÂN. He's a seventy-year-old man in an organisation run by men, you're a sixteen-year-old girl! He won't listen to you.

CARYS. Cos you're doing such a great job of listening to me yourself? Did you speak to him, Miss? Back when you were wild?

SIÂN. Yes.

CARYS. What happens if he believes me?

SIÂN. What?

CARYS. Father Casey? What happens if he thinks this is from God?

SIÂN. –

CARYS. Please, Miss. The Church must have a way to deal with this. I've tried to read up but all the Church stuff is in Latin or Italian. Do you know? Miss?

SIÂN. He'd need to rule out self-harm.

CARYS. How?

SIÂN. I should imagine old women from church would follow you twenty-four-seven.

CARYS. Koolers will be a blast then.

SIÂN. Then there'd probably be a visit from the parish exorcist.

CARYS. The what?

SIÂN. It's still Mr Tomos I think. It always used to be him. He'd decide whether or not you should be treated for possession.

CARYS. As in possession by the Devil?

SIÂN. If they rule that out…

CARYS. If?!

SIÂN. You'd be monitored – for decades. Every single decision you make – relationships, uni, even wearing lipgloss – someone would be commenting on it.

CARYS. Everyone does that here anyway.

SIÂN. This would be different.

SIÂN *scratches her hands again.*

CARYS. Jesus, Miss, don't you have cream for that?

SIÂN. No.

CARYS. You should see a doctor, it's rank.

SIÂN. Name me one person who believes you. Except for your nan.

CARYS. Andy the chippy. He does me a stigmata special when I go in – it's a large bag of chips with gravy and a pickled egg on the side.

SIÂN. Carys! Your stigmata cannot be from God because it's inaccurate.

CARYS. What do you mean, mun?

SIÂN. Your wounds aren't in the right place.

CARYS. What are you talking about?

SIÂN. Jesus wasn't crucified through his hands – the nails would have gone through his wrists. What you have is how crucifixes represent it. They've done it like that since medieval times. It's probably the only way you've ever seen it, but it's not actually true.

CARYS. You're making that up.

SIÂN. No, I'm telling you some facts.

CARYS. So Jesus had the marks on his wrists – why does that matter?

SIÂN. Because if your marks were genuinely from Christ, wouldn't they be in the right place? Do you think God would forget where they banged the nails in?

CARYS. Maybe God put the marks somewhere people would expect them to be so it'd be easier for them to believe. Some really famous stigmatists had marks on their hands. Nan has pictures of them on prayer cards on the fridge.

SIÂN. Maybe they made it up too.

CARYS. Saints don't lie!

SIÂN. You said to me earlier you were doing it yourself!

CARYS. No I never! Stop gaslighting me!

SIÂN. You did! You said it didn't matter whether God had sent it or not for it to be a miracle!

CARYS. It doesn't but he does!

SIÂN. Because it just appears?

CARYS. Yes!

SIÂN. But that might be science!

CARYS. What?

SIÂN. You might have dual-personality syndrome / or...

CARYS. What's that?

SIÂN. It's where you wouldn't remember cutting. Or maybe your body's having a reaction to something and you can't control it. The unconscious mind is really powerful. Look at a blush, eczema even. No one can control how their body responds to emotion and you've been taking on board that image of a crucifixion since you were a child.

CARYS. So have you! Every Catholic has, mun! We don't all go around bleeding! Even those of us who still believe.

SIÂN. What?

CARYS. You never go up for communion on Sundays. Don't think we haven't noticed.

SIÂN *opens the window. They listen.*

SIÂN. Finish that paper for me.

CARYS. You serious?

SIÂN. What else are you going to do?

CARYS. Well according to you I'd normally be cutting myself around now so why don't you hand me some scissors?

SIÂN. They must all believe you to stay this long.

CARYS *writes on the exam paper. The ongoing vibrations from her wrist intensify.* CARYS *quickly clasps her hand over it.*

CARYS. Can I check how many likes the video has now, Miss?

SIÂN. No.

CARYS. Please?

SIÂN. I said no, Carys.

CARYS. It won't take long!

SIÂN. –

CARYS. Miss? Miss!

SIÂN. –

CARYS. Can you check then?

SIÂN. –

Sensing something is happening, SIÂN *goes to the laptop.*

CARYS. Is it loads? Is it more than ten thousand? More than twelve thousand? Thirteen thousand?

SIÂN. Carys, I think you should post saying the video's a hoax.

CARYS. I can't.

SIÂN. Why?

CARYS. I'm on a tech ban.

SIÂN. Very funny. You can use my laptop.

CARYS. No.

SIÂN. Why not?

CARYS. Because I'd be lying! You shouldn't be encouraging that. Lying's a sin.

SIÂN. You wouldn't be lying!

CARYS. Yes I would! Send the video to someone who can analyse it if you want.

SIÂN. How can you stop doing this to yourself if the world is telling you it wants it to be true?

CARYS. Maybe this is God's way of giving you back your faith. Maybe this is all so you'll open your mind and accept you don't always have the answers. I bleed every Friday and it's out of my control. I'm not posting anything.

CARYS *looks at her watch.*

SIÂN. What are you doing? Is that a smart watch? Shit! Hand that over now. Carys! Give me the watch!

CARYS. No way, mun.

SIÂN. Have you had that on the whole time? Carys! Give it to me! You are on school property and when you're on school property, you obey school rules!

CARYS. I'm only on school property because you've kidnapped me.

SIÂN. Give me the watch, Carys!

CARYS. No way! Have you seen what's happening out there? I'm being tagged non-stop! I'm so going to get sixty thousand people liking me, Miss.

CARYS *dashes to the laptop.*

All these people commenting! My mam's just posted! She says she's proud of me. Oh my God!

SIÂN. What?

CARYS. Look! The council chief exec's posted!

SIÂN. What?

CARYS. She says God must have seen the budget sheet and decided to help Merthyr's tourism industry. She wants to stick a grotto on the Gurnos!

SIÂN. Carys.

CARYS. She's speaking to the BBC now in a minute. This is class!

SIÂN. Carys, listen to me!

CARYS. Me listen to you? You should listen to me! They all are! Loads of them are – and not just on the yard now. They can't all be wrong, can they, mun? You should believe too, Miss, help them make it finally stop, that numb feeling all the time cos we're being looked through, ignored. Do you have any idea what it's been like, Miss? To look at my hands each Friday, see blood and think – I must exist, cos that blood comes from inside me? And now they're seeing it too. They can see me.

CARYS *becomes increasingly carefree as the energy from the feed floods into her body.*

SIÂN *quickly moves to the laptop and hurriedly types.*

CARYS *sees* SIÂN *at the laptop, heads towards it.*

Did you just post as me? Miss?

SIÂN. Carys…

CARYS. Oh my God, you… You've signed off with my Memoji! That's me, that's… No one else should use that! Ever! You bitch, Miss!

SIÂN. Do not speak to me like that, Carys!

CARYS. You've silenced me! You pretended to be me so you could silence me!

SIÂN. You uploaded it at lunchtime.

CARYS. So?

SIÂN. Lunchtime here is breakfast time in Latin America – in Mexico, Brazil, Argentina. Countries with millions of devout Catholics! Don't you see? They're not even halfway through the day out there yet. This has the potential to go viral, globally viral. If we don't stop it now, millions of people could soon be watching you on their phones – a girl from Merthyr Tydfil in Wales, bleeding like Jesus Christ. This is me, throwing down safeguarding lightning bolts for you, Carys. We cannot let that happen!

CARYS. I'd love that to happen.

CARYS *deletes the post.*

SIÂN. The second there's a comment from the Church, the whole thing might erupt.

CARYS. Father Casey's commented.

SIÂN. What?

CARYS. He said God moves in mysterious ways. (*To herself.*) No.

SIÂN. Carys?

CARYS. Hmm?

SIÂN. What is it?

CARYS. Nothing. I'm just getting really famous now, that's all.

SIÂN. Let me see.

CARYS. No! Loads of people are saying stuff about me. That's good, Miss. It doesn't matter what they're saying. Everyone will be well jel.

SIÂN *heads to the laptop.*

Miss, don't!

SIÂN. Someone's sent you a death threat!

CARYS. But only for when I'm thirty-four. True stigmatists die at thirty-three like Christ anyway so it's fine.

SIÂN. There are posts here threatening to rape you!

CARYS. Men say stuff to girls like that all the time.

SIÂN. That doesn't make it okay!

CARYS. Better that than them thinking I'm mingin', Miss.

CARYS*'s watch frantically buzzes.*

SIÂN. Give me the watch.

CARYS. As if!

SIÂN. Hand it over.

CARYS. No way!

SIÂN. Don't you get how serious this is?

CARYS. Fuck off! You're just jealous it's me they want to tag, me becoming the superstar. Want to post as me again, do you? Get some attention? Want to live through me now I'm famous? Want to pretend you're still gritty, is it, because the world wants it now? Want to remember what it's like?

CARYS *removes the watch, dangles it in front of* SIÂN *and starts to stalk her around the room.*

Come on then! If you want it that much, mun, fucking take it.

SIÂN. Calm down.

CARYS. I'm sick of this – you saying I'm crazy. Sorry – mentally ill. They don't think that out there, do they? So which of us is crazier? Me, for giving them a miracle, or you for thinking everyone has to think like you? What's the matter, Miss? Did Cardiff make you too posh to scrap me for it? Make you above all that, did it? Your dad was a boxer, wasn't he? Proper Merthyr I heard. How do you think he'd feel about you now if he was still around, thinking you're better than us, keeping us down by trying to stop this being seen? By the world soon now too, Miss! By the fucking world! At least he didn't see you turn into a stuck-up Cardiff cow thinking you're always right, Miss. At least one good thing came out of him killing himself.

SIÂN *throws* CARYS *to the floor, grabs her arm and twists it.*

SIÂN. Don't you ever talk to me like that again, do you hear me? You think this thing needs to be seen? It needs hiding. They're laughing at you, Carys. Can't you hear it? The laughter's echoing through the Beacons from Cardiff and London; people pissing themselves at the thought someone here has anything worth hearing. If you were clever, actually clever, you'd get the fuck out of this place before it takes you by the throat and chokes you. It's ill. This whole town is ill and it infects anyone who stays. His suit is still hanging in their wardrobe. I go into their room at night and take it off the hanger, put it on and hug myself, pretend they're his arms.

CARYS (*in tears*). You're hurting me. Miss, you're really hurting me.

SIÂN *backs away.*

SIÂN. I'm so sorry. I don't know where that came from.

CARYS *runs to the door, bangs on it.*

CARYS (*shouting*). Mr Harris! Mr Harris!

CARYS *heads to the window.* SIÂN *tries to block her.*

SIÂN. No!

CARYS *climbs on the table.*

CARYS (*shouting*). Mam! Mam!

SIÂN. Carys, please. You could fall and hurt yourself.

CARYS. Is that a threat?

SIÂN. What?

CARYS. Are you going to hurt me again?

SIÂN. No! I swear I'm not.

CARYS. Call Mr Williams. Tell him to open the door.

SIÂN. No.

CARYS. You cannot keep me here!

SIÂN. It's for your own good.

CARYS. How is it?

SIÂN. Because we have to fix this or it'll follow you around forever! Please believe me – I know what it'll be like! After we buried my dad, all they did was tell me how I must be feeling and no one once ever stopped to listen. I won't let them do that to you Carys, I won't let them stifle you.

Beat.

CARYS. My God, you… You locked us in here, didn't you? Miss?

Merthyr's not ill! You are. Open the door.

SIÂN *furiously scratches her hands.*

Miss!

SIÂN. I can't!

CARYS. You're treating me like they treated you.

SIÂN *weeps.*

CARYS *watches* SIÂN, *unsure, and listens to singing from outside – 'Myfanwy'.*

SIÂN *unlocks the door.* CARYS *decides not to leave and looks out of the window.*

Mr Harris hasn't moved them yet cos he's out there singing. He's second tenor in Cyfarthfa mixed.

SIÂN *goes to her handbag, from which she pulls out a bottle of water and some paracetamol. She takes them.*

CARYS. I knew you had some.

SIÂN. Take one.

CARYS. No. I don't need to. I wonder if the Merthyr UFO Society's out there. The president put a note through my door once, telling me he'd seen me in his dreams on a spaceship, piloting it in the direction of the Rhondda.

SIÂN. Why did you do it?

CARYS. Do what?

SIÂN. Upload the video.

CARYS. Dunno.

SIÂN. I'm trying to lis/ten.

CARYS. I was cross with you.

SIÂN. Why?

CARYS. You ignored me. So when it was dinner, I borrowed Candice's phone.

SIÂN. How did I ignore you?

CARYS. You asked a question, I stuck up my hand and you picked someone else.

SIÂN. That's school, that's / not…

CARYS. You do it all the time! You picked Olivia Edwards cos she's posh – I know you did. You make me feel invisible.

SIÂN. So you have caused what might soon possibly be a global situation – and I have just ruined my career – because I didn't pick you to answer a question?

CARYS. No. I have caused what might soon possibly be a global situation because you stopped thinking people like me are worth hearing.

SIÂN. If you think that, then I'm so/rry.

CARYS. No – not if I think that. What I think has nothing to do with it. You're sorry or you're not.

SIÂN. I'm sorry. I believe you're hurting. I believe you.

SIÂN *gets a text.*

Father Casey's here.

CARYS. I won't tell them what you did, Miss.

SIÂN. You should. It's okay. Mr Williams wants me to take you to his office. Someone from the crisis team is with them. (*To herself.*) Of course they are.

CARYS. I don't want to go.

SIÂN. What?

CARYS. I don't want to go to the office.

SIÂN. Why?

CARYS. I keep thinking about something your mam said. I told you she believed me, but she believed I wasn't doing it to myself, that's all.

SIÂN. I don't understand.

CARYS. She thought it was this place, Merthyr, screaming at everyone through me. She said I bleed to show how much it hurts here because those with power don't listen and it takes something like this to get them to notice. She said I bleed for men like your dad who can't find work because there's none but just get told they're lazy. She said I bleed for the hungry children, mun, the ones she'd see picking food out of bins on their way to school like seagulls. She told me I was lucky, Miss, because my stigmata's visible and I could at least show them, do something. She said we're all stigmatists here, if our hearts beat for this place. Mine's just visible, that's all.

SIÂN. They already know what it's like here. Trust me, Carys, they do. They just don't care. How can they when they leave coal tips ready to slide down mountains? People matter less than money. And lately, as people died, as so many people died – where were they? And it's all so passive, isn't it? This idea that one day they'll want to help and we should be grateful. Aren't you worth more than that? Look at you. Listen to you. You're worth more than waiting.

SIÂN *gets a text.*

CARYS. Is he seriously tampin' we're not there yet. Miss?

SIÂN. What do you want to do?

CARYS. I know they'll go mental at you, but – I want to go to out there.

SIÂN *scratches her hands.*

They care. They came straight away; they've been here ages. And, the thing is… Maybe me going to them will change stuff, maybe it's a start. Maybe it'll make people see that there's no stigma in being from Merthyr; that I love living here, that that's possible! And not just cos there's some fancy building work happening now, or that we're finally getting a new bus station. I love it cos of the stuff we're told we should feel ashamed about. I love sitting on the steps down the side of Poundland, mun. I love Gethin Woods. And I love seeing memories of what it was like each time I walk down the street. I like smoking by the one wall still standing from the ironworks, knowing my great-great uncle made the family Welsh-cake griddle in there and smuggled it out under his winter coat in July with it hanging around his neck on a rope. I like eating sandwiches by the reservoir each summer and walking past the old synagogue and imagining what it must have been like full. I like seeing trees smash through the inside of chapel windows where I know my great-grandparents and great-great-grandparents sang. Nature's reclaiming them because we're part of nature here. And that means something when it all needs fixing right now. And all that, knowing all that, it makes us part of something great, mun. And where else is so beautiful? Where else do people come together like they do here? Me going there will show people that we're still here for each other, in spite of everything, in spite of all the pain. And me going can let that pain out, get rid of the stigma, for you too, Miss, like a howl. And wouldn't that... Wouldn't that be a miracle?

SIÂN. You don't have to do this, Carys. You don't have to carry the town. You could do anything you set your mind to.

CARYS. I know. But I want to. At least for today.

CARYS *picks up her answers.*

(*Reading.*) 'Diamonds are formed under intense heat and pressure which brings their atoms closer together. This causes a fierce bond and makes each diamond hard and beautiful.' I'm sorry I said you're from Cardiff. You're alright, mun.

CARYS *moves to the door.*

Your dad... It wasn't your fault, Miss. You were sixteen.

SIÂN *can't speak but it's clear how much this means to her.*

CARYS *exits.*

Singing from outside. SIÂN*'s phone rings.*

The singing is interspersed with cheering and chants of CARYS*'s name.*

SIÂN *receives the stigmata.*

End of play.

Glossary

Below is a list of the main Merthyr/Welsh/Wenglish terms and references used in the play.

A470 (pronounced 'A-four-seventy') – a 178-mile road that connects north and south Wales; and it's the road that connects Merthyr to Cardiff.

Abercanaid – a village in Merthyr with a coal-mining past.

A cheeky 'Spoons – a meal in a Wetherspoon pub.

Bampy – grandfather.

Brecon Road – historically the main route into Merthyr from Brecon where the former toll house still stands.

Castle – Cyfarthfa Castle. A Grade I listed building, built by ironmaster William Crawshay II in 1824–25. It later became a school and is now a museum and art gallery.

Crawshay – ironmaster Robert Thompson Crawshay (1817–79), son of William. He was despised locally for the treatment of his workers and women.

'Cwm Rhondda' – a Welsh hymn that features prominently on the soundtrack to the 1941 film *How Green Was My Valley*, an adaptation of Richard Llewellyn's 1939 novel.

Cyfarthfa – an area in west Merthyr with strong links to Merthyr's ironmaking past.

Cyfarthfa Park – the grounds surrounding the castle, now home to a miniature railway.

Dowlais – an area in north-east Merthyr, famous for its ironmaking past.

Express, The – the *Merthyr Express*, Merthyr's weekly newspaper.

Gethin Woods – woodland with stunning views; also a popular place for losing your virginity.

Gower, The – a nineteen-mile long peninsula, famous for its coastline and beaches.

Gruff – a Welsh boy's name, short for Gruffydd; pronounced 'Griff' in English.

Gurnos, The – an estate of council-provided homes, built in the 1950s and expanded significantly in the 1970s.

killin' – really hurting.

Koolers – a nightclub in Merthyr.

mun – used to add emphasis to a sentence.

'Myfanwy' – a Welsh love song, by Merthyr-born composer Joseph Parry.

now in a minute – soon, but not immediately.

old synagogue – a Grade II listed building, built in 1872 and currently being restored as a Jewish Heritage Centre.

Prince Charles – Merthyr Tydfil's hospital.

retail park, The – Cyfarthfa Retail Park, a centre with a mixture of shops, restaurants, etc.

St Dwynwen's Day – 25th January, often seen as the Welsh Valentine's Day. St Dwynwen is Wales's patron saint of lovers and the sister of Tudful, after whom Merthyr Tydfil is named.

tampin' – really angry.

Welsh cakes – round flat cakes with raisins, traditionally cooked on a baking stone or iron griddle.

CARYS'S EXTENDED MONOLOGUE

CARYS

I don't want to go to the office. I keep thinking about something
your mam said. She didn't think I was doing it to myself, Miss,
but she didn't think it comes from God either. She thought it
was this place, Merthyr, screaming at everyone through me. She
said I bleed to show how much it hurts here because those with
power don't listen and it takes something like this to get them to
notice. She said I bleed for men like your dad who can't find
work because there is none but just get told they're lazy. She
said I bleed for the hungry children, mun, the ones she'd seen
picking food out of bins on their way to school like seagulls.
She told me I was lucky, Miss, because my stigmata's visible
and I could at least show them, do something. She said we're all
stigmatists here, if our hearts beat for this place. Mine's just
visible, that's all.

I want to go out there, to them. I want to be with the people,
singing.

It sounds so lush, Miss, their voices together like that – full of
hope. And they're all there, aren't they? My mam, Andy the
chippy, maybe my nan's even left the house with her Zimmer.
I want to stand with them, show them my wounds, hold up my
hands to the crowd and they'll know, mun – they'll know
I bleed for them.

I want them to know they're worth bleeding for. Every week.
Cos they are, Miss. They're worth all that pain. They're the
ones who came – the second they thought I needed help. They
dropped everything to stand outside in a schoolyard and sing,
like we've done here for generations, mun, every time there's
been pain.

And maybe you're right, Miss. Maybe this won't change things
here, maybe no one will ever care, but maybe this is about

showing something different, about me saying to the world that I love living here, that that's possible! And not just cos there's some fancy building work happening now, or that we're finally getting a new bus station. I love it cos of the stuff we're told we should feel ashamed about. I love sitting on the steps down the side of Poundland, mun. I love Gethin Woods.

And I love seeing memories of what it was like each time I walk down the street. I like smoking by the one wall still standing from the ironworks, knowing my great-great uncle made the family Welsh-cake griddle in there and smuggled it out under his winter coat in July with it hanging around his neck on a rope. I like eating sandwiches by the reservoir each summer and walking past the old synagogue and imagining what it must have been like full. I like standing in my back garden and looking out at the mountains, standing to attention and keeping us safe and then looking down and seeing the lavender grow. I like walking up our mountain in summer with my mates, Miss, knowing my bampy did exactly the same thing. I like walking around Cyfarthfa Park and looking up at the one castle window and checking for Crawshay's ghost cos I know when my great aunt was up a ladder cleaning it, that ghost tried to perv up her skirt. And I like seeing trees smash through the inside of chapel windows where I know my great-grandparents and great-great- grandparents sang.

Nature's reclaiming them cos we're part of nature here. And that means something when it all needs fixing right now.

And all that, knowing all that, it makes us part of something great, mun. And where else is so beautiful? Where else do people come together like they do here, like they are right now out there? Me going to them will show everyone that we're still here for each other, in spite of everything, in spite of all the pain.

And yeah, maybe it's dangerous, mun. I'm not stupid. Jesus faced crowds, didn't he, on Palm Sunday. Well, that's my crowd and they're waving smartphones for me instead of palm branches and I get it, Miss. I do. I get in a week or even in a couple of days, mun, they might turn. But me going out there now can let some of that pain out, can't it, get rid of the stigma? For you too, Miss, like a howl. And wouldn't that...

Wouldn't that be a miracle?

SHERMAN THEATR • THEATRE

Artistic Director / Cyfarwyddwr Artistig Joe Murphy
Executive Director / Cyfarwyddwr Gweithredol Julia Barry

Based in the heart of Cardiff, Sherman Theatre is a leading producing house which creates and curates exceptional theatre for the people of Cardiff. Its focus on the development and production of new writing and on nurturing of Welsh and Wales-based artists makes the Sherman the engine room of Welsh theatre. Sherman Theatre tells local stories with global resonance through its productions rehearsed and built under its roof in the capital. The Sherman is a place for everyone. It generates opportunities for the citizens of Cardiff to connect with theatre through inspiring and visionary engagement.

Wedi'i lleoli yng nghanol Caerdydd, mae Theatr y Sherman yn dŷ cynhyrchu blaenllaw sy'n creu a churadu theatr o safon eithriadol ar gyfer pobol Caerdydd. Drwy ei ffocws penodol ar ddatblygu a chynhyrchu gwaith newydd, ac wrth feithrin artistiaid Cymreig, a'r rhai sy'n byw yng Nghymru, mae Theatr y Sherman wedi dod yn bwerdy i theatr yng Nghymru. Drwy'r cynyrchiadau sy'n cael eu hymarfer a'u hadeiladu o dan ei tho yn y brifddinas, mae Theatr y Sherman yn dweud straeon lleol gyda pherthnasedd byd-eang. Mae Theatr y Sherman yn le i bawb. Mae'n creu cyfleoedd i drigolion Caerdydd fedru creu cyswllt â'r theatr trwy ymrwymiad ysbrydoledig a gweledigaethol.

SUPPORT NEW WELSH WRITING

Sherman Theatre is a registered charity. To help us to continue to develop new voices and present bold plays by Welsh and Wales based writers please consider supporting Sherman Theatre with a donation.
Find out more: **shermantheatre.co.uk/support-us/**

CEFNOGWCH YSGRIFENNU NEWYDD CYMRAEG

Mae Theatr y Sherman yn elusen gofrestredig. I barhau y ddatblygiad o leisiau newydd Cymraeg, ac i helpu ni gyflwyno dramau beiddgar gan awduron o Gymru, ystyriwch gefnogi Theatr y Sherman gyda rhodd, os gwelwch yn dda. Rhagor o wybodaeth: **shermantheatre.co.uk/cefnogi/**

To find a full Sherman Theatre staff list and more information please visit our website:
I ddod o hyd i restr lawn o staff Theatr y Sherman a rhagor o wybodaeth ewch i'n gwefan:

SHERMANTHEATRE.CO.UK

 Cyngor Celfyddydau Cymru / Arts Council of Wales The National Lottery® Through the Arts Council of Wales   Cefnogwyd gan Y Loteri Genedlaethol trwy Gyngor Celfyddydau Cymru   Registered Charity Number / Rhif Elusen Cofrestredig 1118364

THEATRE UNCUT

Co-Artistic Director Emma Callander
Co-Artistic Director and Founder Hannah Price

Theatre Uncut creates bold, progressive, uncompromising political theatre. The company is untethered from traditional forms so it can examine burning issues in ways that push the boundaries of what theatre is and what art can achieve.

Created in 2011 in response to the cuts in public spending Theatre Uncut galvanises action, raises awareness and fuels debate by creating political new writing and making it available for everyone, everywhere.

Each year they work with both the world's leading writers and extraordinary new voices to create trailblazing work that examines the world we live in today and make this available for anyone to perform anywhere. So far they have commissioned over 57 playwrights from 14 countries to create responsive work which has been performed in 32 countries across 4 continents.

Theatre Uncut have produced their own work at venues across the UK including the Young Vic, Traverse Theatre and Sherman Theatre. They have collaborated with companies in Turkey, France and Denmark.

In 2018 the Theatre Uncut Political Playwriting Award was created to discover the political playwrights of the future.

www.theatreuncut.com

www.nickhernbooks.co.uk

 facebook.com/nickhernbooks

 twitter.com/nickhernbooks